BASKETBALL LEGENDS

Kareem Abdul-Jabbar

Charles Barkley

Larry Bird

Wilt Chamberlain

Julius Erving

Patrick Ewing

Anfernee Hardaway

Grant Hill

Magic Johnson

Michael Jordan

Shaquille O'Neal

Scottie Pippen

CHELSEA HOUSE PUBLISHERS

BASKETBALL LEGENDS

ANFERNEE HARDAWAY

Jeremy Daniels

Introduction by
Chuck Daly

CHELSEA HOUSE PUBLISHERS
New York   Philadelphia

Produced by Daniel Bial and Associates
New York, New York

Picture research by Alan Gottlieb
Cover illustration by Bill Vann

3 5 7 9 8 6 4 2

Library of Congress Cataloging-in-Publication Data

Daniels, Jeremy.
    Anfernee Hardaway.
    p.   cm. — (Basketball legends)
    Includes bibliographical references and index.
    Summary: A biography of the young scorer whose play helped the
Orlando Magic get to the NBA championship series in 1995.
    ISBN 0-7910-2435-0 (hardcover : alk. paper)
    1. Hardaway, Anfernee—Juvenile literature. 2. Basketball
players—United States—Biography—Juvenile literature. 3. Orlando
Magic (Basketball team)—Juvenile literature.   [1. Hardaway,
Anfernee. 2. Basketball players. 3. Afro-Americans—Biography.]
I. Series.
GV884.A2H247 1996
792.323'092—dc20
[B]   95-42478
                                                    CIP
                                                    AC

CONTENTS

BECOMING A BASKETBALL LEGEND

Chuck Daly

What does it take to be a basketball superstar? Two of the three things it takes are easy to spot. Any great athlete must have excellent skills and tremendous dedication. The third quality needed is much harder to define, or even put in words. Others call it leadership or desire to win, but I'm not sure that explains it fully. This third quality relates to the athlete's thinking process, a certain mentality and work ethic. One can coach athletic skills, and while few superstars need outside influence to help keep them dedicated, it is possible for a coach to offer some well-timed words in order to keep that athlete fully motivated. But a coach can do no more than appeal to a player's will to win; how much that player is then capable of ensuring victory is up to his own internal workings.

In recent times, we have been fortunate to have seen some of the best to play the game. Larry Bird, Magic Johnson, and Michael Jordan had all three components of superstardom in full measure. They brought their teams to numerous championships, and made the players around them better. (They also made their coaches look smart.)

I myself coached a player who belongs in that class, Isiah Thomas, who helped lead the Detroit Pistons to consecutive NBA crowns. Isiah is not tall-he's just over six feet-but he could do whatever he wanted with the ball. And what he wanted to do most was lead and win.

All the players I mentioned above and those whom this series will chronicle are tremendously gifted athletes, but for the most part, you can't play professional basketball at all unless you have excellent skills. And few players get to stay on their team unless they are willing to dedicate themselves to improving their talents even more, learning about their opponents, and finding a way to join with their teammates and win.

It's that third element that separates the good player from the superstar, the memorable players from the legends of the game. Superstars know when to take over the game. If the situation calls for a defensive stop, the superstars stand up and do it. If the situation calls for a key pass, they make it. And if the situation calls for a big shot, they want the ball. They don't want the ball simply because of their own glory or ego. Instead they know—and their teammates know—that they are the ones who can deliver, regardless of the pressure.

The words "legend" and "superstar" are often tossed around without real meaning. Taking a hard look at some of those who truly can be classified as "legends" can provide insight into the things that brought them to that level. All of them developed their legacy over numerous seasons of play, even if certain games will always stand out in the memories of those who saw them. Those games typically featured amazing feats of all-around play. No matter how great the fans thought the superstars were, these players were capable of surprising the fans, their opponents, and occasionally even themselves. The desire to win took over, and with their dedication and athletic skills already in place, they were capable of the most astonishing achievements.

CHUCK DALY, most recently the head coach of the New Jersey Nets, guided the Detroit Pistons to two straight NBA championships, in 1989 and 1990. He earned a gold medal as coach of the 1992 U.S. Olympic basketball team—the so-called "Dream Team"—and was inducted into the Pro Basketball Hall of Fame in 1994.

1

STEPPING UP

Few of the millions of fans watching on television on February 26, 1995, were expecting the Orlando Magic to defeat the Chicago Bulls. The Magic boasted the best record in the Eastern Conference, but they were operating under a huge handicap that day. Their All-Star center, Shaquille O'Neal, who was proving to be the best player in the Eastern Conference, had been suspended as a result of having shoved Eric Montross of the Boston Celtics earlier in the week. Instead of playing O'Neal, the Magic were forced to insert Tree Rollins at the center spot. Brian Hill, the Magic's coach, crossed his fingers in hope that Rollins's 39-year-old body could still survive a full game of running, jumping, and banging against a trio of young Chicago big men.

On top of that, two other members of the Magic's starting five were unable to play. Veter-

Anfernee Hardaway loves to draw in defenders—Scottie Pippen and Toni Kukoc of the Chicago Bulls in this case—and then pass out to an open teammate.

an power forward Horace Grant and guard Brian Shaw were experiencing back spasms and had to watch the game from the bench. And, as if that was not enough, forward Donald Royal sprained his ankle in the first period and had to sit out the rest of the game.

The Bulls were suffering in one way, too. They no longer were the same team that had won three straight NBA championships from 1991 through 1993. Michael Jordan, perhaps the greatest player ever to strap on sneakers, had decided to give up basketball after the 1993 season to test his skills as a baseball player. (On this date, a strike was keeping Jordan from showing off his moderate talents on the ballfield. He would rejoin the Bulls later in the season.)

Still, Chicago was no pushover. The Bulls featured the veteran All-Star Scottie Pippen, Toni Kukoc, a new star recently imported from Europe, and a deep bench. The Bulls were fighting to lock up a top playoff spot and ached to beat the Magic on Orlando's home court—a feat only two other teams had been able to achieve all season long.

If Orlando had any hope of winning, it would have to come from the team's young phenom, Anfernee Hardaway. Hardaway had never been a favorite of the local fans since his arrival from Memphis State University in 1993. Sports radio programs in Orlando went on for hours about how the Magic had been foolish to trade their number one selection in the draft, Chris Webber, to the Golden State Warriors for their number three choice, Hardaway.

But around the NBA, Hardaway was respected for his outstanding skills. A 6'7" point guard, he was often compared with Earvin "Magic" Johnson, the 6'9" guard who changed the way the game of basketball was played. Unusually tall for a playmaker, Johnson led the Los Angeles Lakers to five NBA championships. Many people said there was no comparison between Hardaway and Johnson, but one who disagreed was Magic himself. "Sometimes it's like looking at me," he observed about Hardaway.

Ordinarily, the Magic played a type of game that was easy to categorize. If the perimeter players could not get the ball in to Shaquille O'Neal so he could unleash one of his trademark monster jams, they would let the ball fly from the three-point line. If their shots were a bit off, Shaq was often able to pick up the rebound and stuff it home.

But on this afternoon, Orlando needed a new strategy. Normally, the 24-year-old Hardaway was happy to let O'Neal score the most points and get all the attention. Now, could he change his selfless attitude and become the team leader and big-point scorer?

Chicago jumped out to a sizable lead over the Magic, and early on threatened to put the game away. For much of the second quarter, the Bulls enjoyed a lead of nearly 20 points. But Anfernee Hardaway, better known as Penny, would not let the Bulls relax. He scored seemingly at will whenever he was guarded by only one man— slicing to the basket, or pulling up for a jumper. When the Bulls sent another player to double-team Hardaway, he made beautiful passes to his open teammate. Hardaway also played tough defense and led numerous fast breaks, spotting up for the three-pointer, or making a brilliant no-look pass to the trailer. He rushed through the lane to grab rebounds and made several key steals.

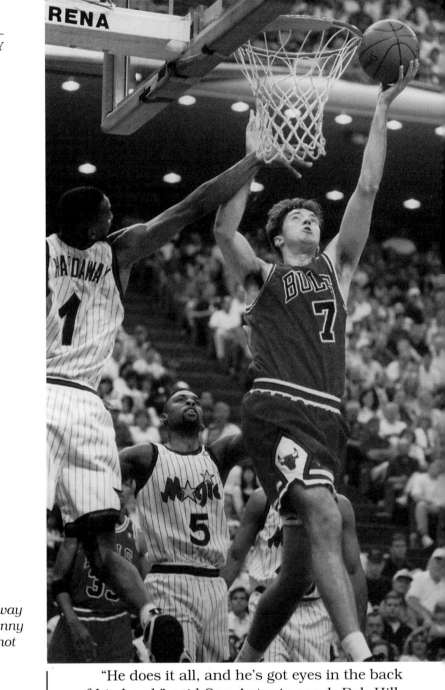

Toni Kukoc has gotten away from his defender, but Penny leaps to make Kukoc's shot more difficult.

"He does it all, and he's got eyes in the back of his head," said San Antonio coach Bob Hill, whose team was victimized by Hardaway for 31 points two weeks later. "If I lived in Orlando, I'd pay double to come and see him play."

By the start of the fourth quarter, Orlando was in even more trouble than at the beginning of the game. Almost all of the available players were in foul trouble. And all were getting tired because of the increased floor time they had to put in. By the time rookie Brooks Thompson fouled out and another Magic player had to sit out the last part of the game with a leg cramp, Orlando was down to six able bodies—five on the floor (including the now huffing and puffing Tree Rollins) and one reserve. The Bulls had all 11 men on their team ready to go.

But with six minutes left to play in the last quarter, the Magic crept back. Led by Hardaway's dead-eye shooting, the Magic reduced Chicago's lead to eight. The Bulls tried to slow the game down, hoping to run out the clock. But they went into a dry spell, seemingly unable to buy a basket. On every possession, a Bull guard slowly walked the ball up court and then dribbled it 30 feet from the basket as the shot clock wound down. Finally, with seconds left, a Bull would heave a desperate shot that Orlando would rebound. The Magic would then lead a rush to their own basket and score quickly.

With two minutes left, the lead was down to five. Two free throws by Orlando's Dennis Scott tied the game at 103-103 with 27 seconds left to play.

The sell-out crowd at Orlando Arena and the television announcers were going crazy as they watched Orlando threaten to steal the game at the last moment. Hardaway had already scored 37 points, just one point below his career high. The Bulls had the ball, but after they came up empty, Orlando also missed its chance to take its first lead since the very opening minutes of the game.

With time for just one last shot, Chicago called timeout to set up a play. Pete Myers inbounded the ball to Toni Kukoc. He slipped, quickly righted himself, slashed to the hoop, and scored easily. But before the ball went into the basket, the referee blew his whistle. The basket did not count. Before Kukoc could recover from his slip, Scottie Pippen had called timeout.

"Scottie thought we were in trouble and called a timeout," said Coach Phil Jackson after the game. "Actually, we were on our way to the basket. Some unfortunate set of circumstances surrounded that."

When play resumed, there were seven seconds left in regulation. Orlando was hoping just to stop Chicago from scoring so they could go to overtime, even if they might not have the manpower to continue to play the Bulls even up.

The Magic looked for the ball to end up in Kukoc's hands again, and when the players hit the court, Orlando recognized Chicago's offensive set. It was one the Bulls had used in a playoff game against the New York Knicks the season before. Sure enough, Kukoc made a beeline to the free-throw line, took the inbound pass, and wheeled around to take the final shot.

But Hardaway and Nick Anderson collapsed on Kukoc defensively. Anderson came from behind and got a hand on the ball. Hardaway picked up the ball and started dribbling toward the basket at the other end of the court.

"I knew I had enough time to get there," Hardaway said later. "I was afraid somebody might foul me, so I was just trying to go as fast as I could."

"Penny shot down the court like a deer," said Dennis Scott afterwards. "I thought, 'No one is going to catch him, not even the clock.'"

The horn ending the game sounded less than a second after the ball had settled through the strings of the net. Along with 7 rebounds and 7 assists, Hardaway had upped his personal best as a pro to 39 points, and the Bulls had to leave the court shaking their heads.

"I'm a big believer that you find out a lot about people's character when you're confronted with adversity, and we had a lot of adversity [in this game]," said Magic coach Brian Hill.

"The top players can adjust their game to the situation," Hardaway said afterwards. "That's what I try to do every night. If points are what we need, I can provide them. But many times, we have other people to do that. My role is to do whatever is needed."

"The only one I would compare him to is Jordan," said David Robinson, who would win the regular season's Most Valuable Player Award. "Jordan has that kind of athletic ability to overwhelm people. Hardaway is developing some of those skills that already make him so tough to handle."

Hardaway downplayed the compliment. "People are always going to make comparisons," he said. But Charles Barkley, a former MVP winner with the Phoenix Suns, went even further than Robinson. "You know what I think? I think the kid from Orlando, Anfernee Hardaway, he's the one that when it's all said and done is going to be the best."

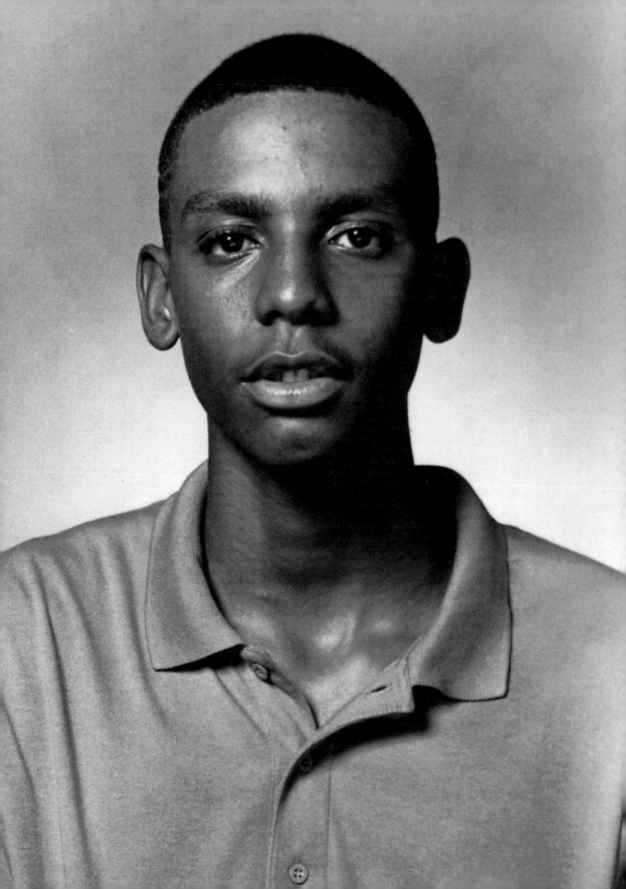

2

PWEDDY BABY

Anfernee Hardaway grew up poor. His grandmother worked as a sharecropper in rural Arkansas. For every long day she spent under the burning sun picking cotton, she earned $2.50. One evening in the summer of 1943, Louise Hardaway and her two young sons were trudging home after another tough day in the fields. She was five months pregnant with her third child when a car came by.

"There was three men in it, " she recalled in her deep southern accent. "White fellers. One of them chucked a brick and hit me in my stomach. Felt I was gonna die." But her spirit kept her determined. "I wasn't gonna die like no dog in the road."

When Louise's husband, Sylvester, returned from his farming job, he found his wife curled up in agony. He was so angry he ran outside and beat his hands against a tree until they were raw and bleeding.

Fae Hardaway named her son Anfernee because she knew another boy with that name and she liked the way it sounded.

Four months later, Louise gave birth to a daughter. Gloria was a healthy child, but Louise never fully recovered from the attack. A doctor advised her to get away from the cotton fields—where the heat made her sick—and move to the city. Six years later, she and Sylvester saved up enough to put a $365 payment down on a decrepit, three-room house in Memphis, Tennessee. On January 1, 1950, the Hardaways moved into the house at 2977 Forrest Avenue.

The narrow house was in terrible shape. It had only three small rooms in shotgun style—one lined up after another. The floors had holes in them; the walls were lined with tar paper. The bathroom was a hole. In a neighborhood of poor houses, this one was one of the worst. "I decided one day I was going to get it in living condition for me," Louise said. "Not for the king of England, but for me and mine."

Louise found work cleaning and cooking in rich people's homes. Although the neighborhood remained rundown, Louise gradually built up her house to be one of the nicest around.

A year later, Louise gave birth to her fourth child, Fae. Five years later, in 1956, Louise and Sylvester separated. It became even more difficult for her to provide for herself and her family, but Louise was ever determined. She found work at small jobs helping others. From 1965 to 1978, she worked in the cafeteria of an elementary school without missing a day.

In 1972, Fae gave birth to Anfernee. She was unmarried and only 19 years old. "Penny was brought here from the hospital," Louise told Ralph Wiley of *Sports Illustrated*. "Fae was just a child herself. She wanted to name him Gold-

en, after his daddy, Eddie Golden. I said, 'Naw.'
I gave him my name, Hardaway."

"When I was in school at Lester High," Fae
said, "there had been a boy named Anfernee. I
always thought it was such a beautiful name.
People think I don't know how to spell Anthony.

"His nickname, Penny? That came from
mama. She called him Pretty, but in the country, that comes out 'Pweddy.' People just took it
from there."

Penny had huge hands when he was born.
They "were so big, it looked like he was wearing
gloves," his mother recalled.

Young single mothers are often unprepared
emotionally for the rigors of parenthood. Many
of them are essentially children themselves. They
may have all the good wishes in the world, hoping that having a child will gain them respect
and a sense of themselves, hoping that they will
have something they can love and treasure in
life.

But then the troubles come. Usually, there's
not much money around. Single mothers do not
always do well in school so they do not have good
prospects for getting a good job. Even if they find
a good job, who will look after their children while
they are away at work?

Fae went back to high school and graduated a year later after Penny was born. He lived
with his mother until he was six years old. But
then Fae married and left for Oakland, California, hoping to find work as a singer and start a
new life. "She wanted to leave Penny with her
sister, Gloria," Louise said. "But I told Fae to
leave my baby here with me.

"Penny was six years old before he saw his
daddy," she continued. "It was that long before

I saw him myself. He said, 'Let me have him.' I said, 'Hell naw.' Hadn't bought him a diaper, and now you want to be a daddy?"

"It was hard at first because I felt no one really wanted me," Penny recalled. "But my grandmother proved that she loved me and cared about what happened to me."

Statistics show children of single mothers are much more prone to becoming addicted to drugs, engaging in criminal behavior, going to jail, or dying young.

No one escapes coming from a broken family unscarred. But Penny Hardaway is a survivor. He knows his life has turned out much better than the lives of many of his friends and schoolmates.

Still, he cannot forget what he suffered as a child. "As I got older, I was wondering when my mom was going to come home," he said. "My grandmother was there for me and I love her a lot. But I also wanted to see my mom and dad because I missed out on a lot of things when I was growing up. She couldn't take me to the ballgame, she couldn't take me to do anything because she was so old. But she tried her best to. When I got older and when my mom called, I'd say, 'When are you gonna come home? When are you gonna come and see me?' It hurt a lot."

Penny never accepted his loneliness, but he learned how to make peace with the life he was leading. He was quiet and shy and did things on his own. Once, while visiting an uncle, the phone rang and Penny answered. He recognized the voice on the line: it was his father, who did not recognize his son's voice. Without betraying how he felt inside, Penny handed the phone to his uncle and went outside to play. Later he met his father several times, but he never formed a relationship with him.

Louise's little house on Forrest Avenue was too small to contain a growing boy. There was usually only one book in the house, a Bible. Penny spent most of his free time in the streets around his home—streets filled with teenagers who skipped school, engaged in thievery, and took drugs.

Louise worried constantly about Penny. She could watch him and try to keep him away from the wrong influences. But during the summers, when school was closed, she could not supervise his activities during the day. "Every boy he was raised up with on this street seem like they've been in jail or the workhouse for robbing and stealing," Louise said. "One of them little boys ended up getting life. For a long time, I didn't let [Penny] out of my sight. 'Course, I couldn't pick his friends."

She instilled a strong sense of right and wrong into the growing Penny. The two went to church every Sunday. When Louise did not have the energy to go, Penny went by himself. He stayed away from the neighborhood toughs selling crack.

Hardaway was a star basketball player in high school. As a senior, he was considered one of the top ten college picks in the country.

His home away from home was the nearby basketball courts, where he spent most of his time when he was not in school.

"I played on those goals eight and nine hours a day, since I was eight years old," Hardaway said. "It got to where boys came, played, went home, ate, came back, and I'd still be there playing. Mostly, I played by myself."

But when the sun went down, Louise ordered Penny home. "My friends were all out there playing, and I was in the house saying, 'Man, I can't wait to get old enough to get out of here," Penny remembered. "My teachers used to say, 'You're going to thank her one day.' And I do now."

By the time he entered junior high, Penny had become a terrific athlete. He was tall, graceful, and lightning fast. He could shoot, pass, and control a game. He did things with a basketball no one had seen since a schoolboy named Earvin Johnson created magic on the courts of Lansing, Michigan, in the late 1970s. As a 15-year-old, Magic Johnson set a city record by scoring 54 points. A 14-year-old Hardaway made comparisons inevitable when in one game against high school players he scored 70 points.

Larry Finch, the Memphis State University coach, hoped that Hardaway would want to stay in his home town to attend college.

Penny was fast becoming a celebrity. The best-known person in Memphis, Tennessee, was Elvis Presley. But by the time Penny's high school career began, people were starting to say that Memphis had a second king—with a better first step.

Hardaway had to walk two miles every day to get to Treadway High School. Meanwhile, scouts from far and wide flew and drove there to see what the young man could do. "Anfernee can absolutely do it all—drive, post up, handle the break, play defense," said Craig Esherick, an assistant coach at Georgetown University who tried to recruit Penny. "Going one-on-one with Anfernee is no way to stay healthy."

It would have been understandable if Penny had gotten a swelled head from all the praise. *Sporting News* magazine named him one of the top ten high school basketball players in the country. "He was very quiet, to himself, not braggadocious or anything like that," said Garmer Currie, Jr., Hardaway's high school coach. Of course, Penny's grandmother would not have allowed any excess pride.

3

TIGER PENNY

During Anfernee Hardaway's senior high school season, the phone at 2977 Forrest was ringing 40 to 50 times a day from recruiters at top colleges across the country. And then something happened to make those inquiries stop. Penny scored poorly on the American College Testing (ACT) exam. According to the rules of the National College Athletics Association (NCAA), all students must maintain a grade-point average of at least 2.0 and score at least 700 on the SAT or 18 on the ACT. If they do not, they become ineligible to play college ball.

This rule, known as Proposition 48, was highly controversial, but all agreed that at least it tried to address a serious problem. Many colleges and universities were accepting students into their athletic programs who were incapable of doing the academic work. These "students" did not graduate; they simply played ball during their years of eligibility. If they could not turn

Hardaway was a star at Memphis State as soon as he got to play for the Tigers.

pro afterwards—and very few could—they returned to their homes with no skills, no degree, no preparation for the rest of their life. Proposition 48 was an attempt to make sure that all students and all colleges took the academic part of college seriously.

With Hardaway no longer eligible to play basketball as a freshman, a lot of universities backed off. His high school average had also been a troubling 2.2—barely good enough by Proposition 48 standards. Many colleges doubted he could keep up his academic standing and were afraid to give a scholarship to someone who might never be able to play for them.

"I can hoop with anybody you name," Penny said. "But I could not pass that ACT. I took it four times. I think I did better each time. But not good enough."

Memphis State University was precisely one of those colleges at which Proposition 48 was aimed. Dana Kirk put together a highly successful basketball program, winning nearly three-quarters of all the games he coached. But of the 60 full-scholarship athletes to play for Kirk in seven years, only six graduated. Few of his players were ever drafted by the NBA, and none enjoyed major careers.

In 1985-86, MSU had one of its best basketball seasons ever, going to the Final Four in the NCAA championship. But only two of the 12 players on the roster ended up graduating, and Kirk was let go.

"[We] rationalized that we had been giving those kids a chance to go to college. That was a crock," said Charlie Cavagnaro, the athletic director at MSU. "We finally came to the conclusion that we had to graduate them."

Memphis State hired Gina Pickens to act as academic counselor for the football and basketball players. Her job was to ensure that the athletes kept up their work and had someone to turn to in case they ever had problems. She was originally given a desk and a small room, but she experienced such success—eight of the first 10 basketball seniors graduated—that three other counselors were subsequently hired.

Penny could have gone to a junior college in order to bring his grades up and play ball at the same time. Instead, he decided to pay to attend Memphis State and stay near his family. But he was not allowed to play for the Tigers or even practice with them for a full year. He could only practice by himself or play with friends. Meantime, he devoted himself to hitting the books. He took more classes than Proposition 48 required of him and earned a grade-point average of just under 3.0—much better than the 2.0 GPA necessary. "Academically, he did an outstanding job," said Pickens.

Showing that he could pull up his grades was a maturing act for Penny. "You know, there was not anybody telling me, 'That's OK. Just wait 'til next year,'" he said. "They said, 'You're dumb....'

"Brothers from the hood do it, too. I went over to this girl's house. A guy came in and said, 'Oh yeah, you that dumb ballplayer.' He's known for selling cocaine. But I'm the dumb one, right?"

Penny faced another serious hurdle while he was a freshman. In April 1991, he and a friend were standing outside the house of Hardaway's cousin, LaMarcus Golden, a point guard for the University of Tennessee. Four men drove up, pulled out guns, and ordered them to lie facedown on the ground. They took a portable phone from Penny's friend, Terry Bernard Starks. They took money and jewelry from both Starks and Hardaway. As Penny lay on the pavement, he kept thinking, "'He's going to shoot me in my back, he's going to shoot me in my head.'"

Hardaway called upon his religious upbringing. 'I was just laying there, just praying that he wouldn't shoot me." He made a promise: "Hopefully, I will get out of this and adjust my ways of going out and my way of doing things."

The robbers jumped in their car and started to drive off. Suddenly, the car stopped about 20 yards down the street. The robbers started shooting. A bullet hit Penny in the right foot, breaking three toe bones.

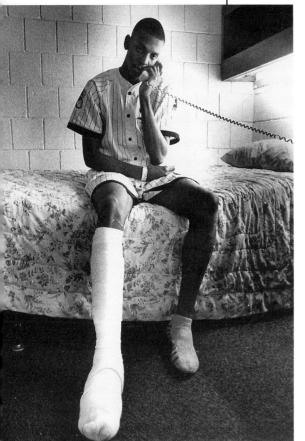

Penny takes a sympathy call and wears a cast on his foot after having been shot by burglars.

At first the doctors would not remove the bullet because they feared damaging a nerve. They put his foot in a cast and warned Penny that he might not be able to play basketball again. "I had to wait 30 minutes to see the X-ray and find out it wasn't as bad as they thought," Hardaway said. "But in those 30 minutes, I tried to think about how life would be without basketball."

Eventually the robbers were caught and sent to prison. The press played up the story. Some reporters suggested that Hardaway, by hanging out with questionable friends in dangerous locations, was at least partially to blame for his situation.

Facing death like that changes a person. The dangerous streets had threatened to take the lives of several of his friends, and now they had almost taken his. Penny learned that he could take nothing for granted. All that he had could be taken away in an instant. Having a healthy body is a temporary gift: an injury could cut short a career at any moment, a bullet can come and wipe out everything you've ever worked for, ever hoped for.

Penny learned to "treasure life" and make every day important. During his sophomore season, he continued to apply himself to his studies. He owned the highest grade-point average of all the basketball players and even made the dean's list. He announced he would major in secondary education.

By November, the bullet had shifted to a position where it could be removed safely. Hardaway was then already working out with the Tigers basketball team.

Penny had now reached his full height of 6'7".

In his first game as a Tiger, MSU inaugurated its new arena, the Pyramid, which would soon be known as "The Tomb of Doom." Twenty thousand rabid rooters came out on December 9, 1991, to see if the young phenom could live up to his billing.

He could. Penny had 18 points, 15 rebounds, 6 assists, 4 blocks, and 4 steals. With seven seconds left in the fourth quarter, he hit a three pointer to send the game into overtime. DePaul University still won the game 92-89, but Hardaway's performance was thrilling.

"I know he's going to be a great player," said a happy Tigers coach Larry Finch.

In the following days, Penny became Mr. Everything for the MSU Tigers. He jumped center to start the game. He set up as point guard. He played a little at forward. He crashed the boards for rebounds. He hit three pointers. He handed out assists and picked opponents' pockets for steals. In his first year on the team, Memphis State made it to the Final Eight of the NCAA tournament. Penny was voted the Great Midwest Player of the Year.

Hardaway's play was so impressive that he had the signal honor of being invited to scrimmage against the "Dream Team," the U.S. Olympic basketball team, in the summer of 1992. Going up against such all-time greats as Michael Jordan, Magic Johnson, Larry Bird, Charles Barkley, Scottie Pippen, Clyde Drexler, and John Stockton would be the ultimate test for any player—and in the Olympics, the Dream Team showed that no one from any other country could play them evenly for as long as 15 minutes.

Hardaway was not fazed by all the greatness he was facing. Larry Bird of the Boston Celtics was impressed enough to call him "Mr. Defense"—and this nickname came from a man who was not used to being stopped by anyone.

For years, Penny had been compared to Magic Johnson. Now, Penny was given a chance to play against the man. Johnson came away saying, "At times, I thought I was looking in a mirror, he reminds me of myself so much.

"I was very impressed with his decision-making," Johnson continued. "We had fun talking a little stuff to each other, him coming back at me, I'm going back at him. That was fun. He took it all in stride, and he still maintained his game. See, usually when you're talking stuff to a young guy, now he's going to try to take the next 10 shots, try to come at me. He never tried to do that. He just took the shot that he had or passed it off. I was very impressed with his floor game and his smarts."

Penny also played at the Olympic Festival, where his team won the gold medal. One of his teammates was someone he was glad to make friends with. "I gave Shaquille O'Neal a no-looker on the break," Penny said. "He tore down the rim. The fans all said, 'Oooh!'"

For his second season at MSU, Hardaway only got better. He led the Great Midwest Conference in scoring, rebounding, and minutes played. He was second in assists and third in blocks. In five games, he scored over 30 points, including a high of 37 against Brigham Young University. And yet he preferred not to be the big scorer. Coach Finch screamed at him all the time to pass less and shoot more. "I've never seen a player as unselfish as Penny," Finch said.

Finch's bigger problem was getting the rest of the team to keep up with Hardaway. Several times a game, a brilliant pass from Penny would skip off an unprepared teammate's hand or go out of bounds. Opponents would double or triple

Bryan Brown of Western Kentucky University is about to take a spill trying to defend against Hardaway. Western Kentucky ousted the Tigers in the 1993 NCAA tournament.

Memphis State retired Hardaway's jersey, although he only played two years for the team. His mother, grand-mother, and coach stood by Penny during the emotional ceremony.

team Penny, and his teammates did not always get over to help out.

"You can see the difference in the ballclub when we take the pressure off Penny," Kenny Allen said. "He does everything. But now he can kind of control the flow and stop doing so much work. He's a phenomenal player. Without him, we'd be a different ballclub."

Penny was the only Division I player to rank in the top six in his conference in points, rebounds, assists, steals, and blocks. On January 18, 1993, he was named *Sports Illustrated*'s Player of the Week when he averaged a triple double: 27.3 points, 14.0 rebounds, and 10.0 assists in three games against Georgia State University, Vanderbilt University, and DePaul University—all wins for Memphis State.

Memphis State was ranked number 10 in their division when "March Madness" rolled around. They were pitted against the University of Western Kentucky, ranked number 7, in the first round of the NCAA championship series. Western Kentucky had no stars the magnitude of Penny, but they had fashioned a 24-5 season. They gave the Tigers a quick exit, beating them 55-52.

Hardaway had again been voted the Great Midwest Player of the Year in his junior year. In the last home game of that season, Tigers fans stood and chanted, "One more year!" They knew that Hardaway was likely going to give up his last year of eligibility and turn pro. Hardaway had already been besieged by hundreds of phone calls from agents, all of them promising him millions of dollars if he left college and made himself available to the NBA draft.

Penny gave the fans something to remember. He showed off his versatility in that game against St. Louis University, playing three different offensive positions, making beautiful passes, and flashing his usual tight defense. He also scored 31 points on only 12 shots, as the Tigers won 75-72. Penny was honored by being named a first-team All-American at the end of the year along with Calbert Cheaney of Indiana University, Bobby Hurley of Duke, Chris Webber of the University of Michigan, and Jamal Mashburn of the University of Kentucky.

Although Memphis State did not have a powerhouse team or basketball program, all the scouts and general managers knew that if Hardaway wanted to turn pro, he'd be a top pick in the draft. Larry Bird had put all the general managers on alert when he said, "I think Anfernee Hardaway is the best college player."

4

THE STEAL OF
THE DRAFT

By an amazing stroke of luck, the Orlando Magic had the first pick in the NBA draft two years in a row. In 1992, they, along with all the other worst teams, coveted one player: Shaquille O'Neal. Critics might point out that O'Neal was not as polished and experienced as Christian Laettner of Duke University or Alonzo Mourning of Georgetown University. But O'Neal was the biggest, strongest, and fastest center to be joining the pros in years. When the draw for the draft was held and Orlando came away with the number one pick, everyone knew whom they would choose.

In the 1991-92 season, Orlando won 21 and lost 61 games. After the arrival of Shaq, they improved hugely to a 41-41 record. That tied them with Indiana for the eighth and last play-

In a controversial draft day trade, the Orlando Magic used their number one pick to choose Chris Webber (left) and then swapped him to the Golden State Warriors who had used their third selection to pick Anfernee Hardaway.

35

The Magic made the playoffs for the first time in their history in 1994. But the Indiana Pacers, in a major upset, swept them out of the post-season. Here Haywoode Workman has beaten Penny and goes to the basket against Orlando backup center Tree Rollins.

off spot, but because the Pacers had beaten the Magic in their head-to-head matchups that year, Indiana got to continue their season and Orlando stayed home.

Somehow, that turned into Orlando's biggest piece of luck. Because they missed the playoffs, their name was placed in a lottery along with the names of the teams with losing records to ensure that the worst clubs would get a chance at the best players coming into the pros. Because the Magic had the best record of all the lottery teams, Orlando had the longest odds against getting the first pick—one in 66. But luck was on their side.

This time, the number one pick was not so obvious. Curiously, none of the top choices were seniors. Analysts seemed to lean to Chris Webber as the best prospect available. A center for the University of Michigan, Webber was the leader of the "Fab Five," a group of unheralded freshmen who had amazingly led Michigan to the finals of the NCAA championship. At 6'10", he was burly, like O'Neal, with good quickness. Orlando fans drooled at the thought of Webber playing forward next to O'Neal. No other team would ever get a rebound, they surmised.

There were three other top prospects. Jamal Mashburn of Kentucky was an outstanding shooter and ballhandler. Sean Bradley of Brigham Young, at 7'6", was the tallest player ever to be a top choice, but his lack of experience—he had spent his last two years of college serving as a missionary, as required by his Mormon religion—made him a huge question mark. And there was Anfernee Hardaway, who boasted less of a national reputation because he played for Memphis State.

On draft day, Orlando dropped a bomb on the basketball world. They picked Chris Webber and then traded him to the Golden State Warriors for the rights to Anfernee Hardaway and three first-round picks in 1996, 1998, and 2000. Immediately, the sports radios in central Florida were filled with the complaints of disappointed fans who could not believe their team had let such an attractive player as Webber slip through their fingers. Even *Sports Illustrated* opined that the Warriors were the big winners in this switch. "No one thought the Warriors could land the big man they needed without breaking up their nucleus, but they did just that."

Originally, Orlando was not very interested in Penny. They had asked him to come in for a tryout, and he had not performed at the top of his game. Hardaway asked the Magic for the chance to try again, and he had an ally in Shaquille O'Neal. At the second meeting, Hardaway "blew us away," said Magic director of player personnel, John Gabriel.

"He was spectacular," said team president Dick DeVos. "He impressed everyone in the building and within a half-mile of the building."

"Not to knock Golden State, but I'm going to love playing with Shaquille O'Neal," said an equally happy Penny Hardaway.

Webber won Rookie of the Year honors, but has not yet turned into a great player. He became unhappy with his coach at Golden State, sulking and poisoning the team atmosphere. Coach Don Nelson became sick and was eventually let go from his position, in large part because he and Webber could not see eye to eye. Within a year, Golden State gave up on Webber entirely, trading him to the Washington Bullets.

Penny asked Kevin and Carl Poston to be his agents, and they negotiated an amazing deal for Penny. Orlando agreed to pay $68 million over 13 years for Hardaway's services, an average salary of over $5 million per year. With incentives, the deal could be worth close to $100 million. In addition, the Postons signed a lucrative sneaker and apparel deal with Nike for approximately $8 million.

Soon after signing the contract—just before training camp opened—Penny bought a $150,000 house for his mother and grandmother. Louise Hardaway refused to part with her old house, though. She had one of her 15 grandchildren move into it. Penny also bought himself a sportscar and a large house by a lake in Orlando.

Hardaway was suddenly rich and famous. Becoming a celebrity was difficult, however, for a sensitive young man such as Anfernee Hardaway. Some people love the glare of the spotlight, the media always aiming cameras at them and sticking microphones in their face, asking for a quote. Of all Penny's teammates, only Shaquille O'Neal gets more attention. And Shaq clearly loves the limelight. He thrives on having people staring at him wherever he goes.

Sometimes, the attention makes Hardaway seem all the more shy. One night, he wanted to celebrate after a big victory. He drove to a dance hall in Orlando, but the crush of people was too great. Other stars might have pushed in, letting the awed crowd make way for them. Anfernee simply decided to get back in his car and go to bed. He did not even want to go anywhere else. "I like my privacy," he said. "I'm not the guy who likes to go out on the town every night."

"I don't know if Penny's too sensitive," said Brian Shaw, Hardaway's best friend on the Magic. "He's always dealing with outsiders who want to uncover something about him. When I was in Boston, I remember Larry Bird telling me once he hadn't been to a shopping mall in 13 years. It shouldn't be like that."

But Penny is not totally averse to the lure of fame. In 1993, he took a call from Hollywood and agreed to appear in the basketball film "Blue Chips." It helped that Shaquille O'Neal was also starring in the movie along with actor Nick Nolte.

While Hardaway was out in Los Angeles for the filming, he became friends with Jaleel White, the actor who played Steve Urkel in the television show "Family Matters." During the 1995 playoffs, Jaleel White stayed in Hardaway's house, playing video games, eating pizza, and generally hanging out. "He should be on my taxes," Hardaway joked.

Greg Moore and Carlos Jackson, friends of Hardaway's since his freshman year at Memphis State, also hang out a lot with him. Hardaway asked Moore to be his personal assistant, and Moore recently moved down the block to be closer to his friend and boss.

Coach Brian Hill was worried that Hardaway's youth and inexperience would mean that it would take time before Penny started to pay dividends. Another question was Penny's weight. In college, he had been reed-thin at 195 pounds, and he had only put on another five pounds since then.

Did Hardaway have the stamina to run and bang with the big boys of the NBA? Could he keep up his energy to compete over the long schedule?

Hill soon recognized that Penny was the team's best point guard. Scott Skiles had been the starter, and people around the league rated him one of the best. But by midseason, Hill had upgraded Hardaway to that position, and Skiles came off the bench. Skiles later asked to be traded, and Orlando obliged by sending him to Washington.

During his first year with Orlando, Hardaway led the Magic in assists and steals, was second in scoring, and third in rebounds. He was runner-up to Chris Webber in Rookie of the Year Award voting.

Meanwhile, Hardaway formed a terrific partnership with Shaquille O'Neal. Hardaway's versatility drew defenders away from the basket, which helped O'Neal to rule the paint. "It's great playing with Shaquille," Penny said. "I think it's a combination that could rule the '90s."

Orlando had its best season ever during 1993-94, wining 50 games. Around the NBA, the question was: how long would it be before Orlando, an expansion team that had played its first game in 1989, won the championship?

The Magic's opponent in the first round of the 1994 NBA playoffs was the Indiana Pacers. Orlando had the home-court advantage because Indiana had won three games fewer than the Magic that season.

Hardaway posted good numbers in the series against the Pacers. He led his team in assists and steals, was second in blocked shots and points, and third in rebounds. He shot a solid 5 of 11 from beyond the three-point circle. But

Indiana shocked everyone by bumping off Orlando in three straight games. The first two were decided by one and two points, respectively. Indiana singed Orlando, 99-86, in the last game.

The Pacers were ousted by the New York Knicks, the eventual Eastern Conference winners. Hardaway and the Magic knew they would need to gain experience and maturity in order to reach the next level of excellence.

5

CLOSER AND CLOSER

Hardaway showed a new-found serious-
ness after his rookie season. He had created a
book on all opposing players he faced, detailing
what their moves were and what his strategies
should be in order to shut them down. "I try to
study everybody in the league because I want to
get an upper hand on them," Penny said. "I
looked at a lot of my [game] tapes from last year.
Being a rookie, I didn't know much."

After being ushered out of the playoffs so
rudely in 1994, the Magic came back determined
to show that they truly were among the elite
teams in the NBA.

They made one important pickup during the
offseason, wooing veteran power forward Horace
Grant away from the Chicago Bulls. Now Shaq
would have another strong rebounder and phys-
ical presence at the post position. And Orlando
would have a proven winner, an athlete with

*Hardaway holds the trophy for winning the Most
Valuable Player award during the 1994 Rookie All-
Star Game. Penny scored 22 points in the game.*

extensive playoff experience to guide them in the big games.

But just as important a change was the maturing of Orlando's contributing players, Dennis Scott and Nick Anderson. Scott was rapidly becoming the league's best three-point shooter, and Anderson was a defensive gem, capable of stopping the likes of Michael Jordan and Reggie Miller. All the players were getting to know each other better, and the extra year of pro experience was a real boon to the youngest Magic blue chippers, Shaquille O'Neal and Anfernee Hardaway.

The harder Hardaway worked, the more he allowed himself to dream how good he could become. "One day I want to be the best player in the NBA," he admitted. "I got stepping stones to get there. I can't be going out to nightclubs, going drinking or whatever [and expect] to accomplish my dream. I try to go home after every game, relax, just study [the tapes] and try to be the best."

Orlando romped through the regular season, proving almost unbeatable at home. They finished with the best record in the Eastern Conference, guaranteeing them home-court advantage for at least the first three rounds of the playoffs. They were the second-fastest expansion team to win their division; only the Milwaukee Bucks—after they drafted Kareem Abdul-Jabbar—went from nowhere to the top faster. Shaquille enjoyed another monster season, leading the league in scoring and rating high in rebounds and shooting percentage. Penny also was outstanding, doing whatever his team needed in order to win.

Orlando's first opponent in the 1995 playoffs were the fabled Boston Celtics who had won more games than any other team in NBA history. Led by such greats as Bill Russell and Bob Cousy, Boston won an astonishing eight championships in a row starting in 1957. With Larry Bird, Kevin McHale, and Robert Parish, the Celtics had also won four in a row from 1984-1987. But none of these stars were still with the team in 1995. Nor was Reggie Lewis, a superstar in the making, who had just died of a heart condition. All told, the Celtics were seriously undermanned against the Magic. The Celtics' only star was the aging Dominique Wilkins, who for many years had led the league in amazing shots. When he played for Atlanta, he had been dubbed "The Human Highlight Film," but he had never been able to lead the Hawks to a championship, and was only going to last in Boston this one year before heading off to play basketball in Greece.

Penny was not only Shaquille O'Neal's teammate, he was also his costar. This scene from the movie "Blue Chips" also featured Nick Nolte (second from left) and Matt Nover (second from right).

Orlando won the first game, 124-77, the worst defeat Boston had suffered in their history. But in the second game, Boston came back to stun the Magic in Orlando, 99-92. "At the end, they made big shots. They deserved to win the game," Hardaway said afterwards.

The teams then headed for Boston, where it had been announced that the venerable Garden was going to be torn down after the series. The

Celtics had a tradition of being unbeatable in big games on their home court. The parquet floor there was probably the roughest such surface in the NBA, and Celtic players knew how to accommodate the unusual bounces that sometimes resulted. Moreover, the Celtics could always get inspiration by looking with pride up with to the rafters where numerous conference and championship banners hung, along with the retired jerseys of many great players.

Was Orlando about to self-destruct like it did against Indiana one year earlier? If the Celtics could win the next two games on their home court, they would oust the heavily favored Magic. What's more, Orlando had won only two of the last 12 games it had played in Boston and had also lost its last seven games on the road.

Yet the Magic won the first game played in Boston, as Hardaway soared to block a shot by Dominique Wilkins at a key juncture of the fourth quarter. Then, with 16 seconds left in Game 4, Wilkins missed a free throw that would have tied the score.

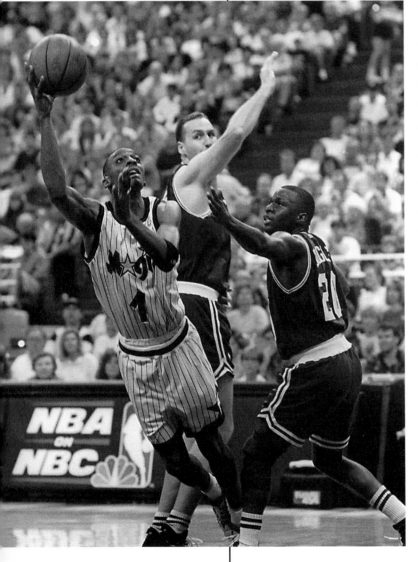

Despite being fouled, Anfernee Hardaway has managed to squeeze between Boston's Dino Radja and Sherman Douglas. He made the shot and the free throw as Orlando beat the Celtics in the first round of the 1995 playoffs.

Horace Grant grabbed the rebound, was fouled by Dino Radja, and sank both free throws to clinch the series for the Magic.

"This building is the best building in the history of basketball," Penny said afterwards. "This will go a long way, because we were the last team to win here."

Up next were the Chicago Bulls, who had just beaten Alonzo Mourning, Larry Johnson, and the rest of the Charlotte Hornets. Chicago, winner of three NBA championships in 1991, 1992, and 1993, was sparked by the late-season return of Michael Jordan. "His Airness" had given up his attempt at a baseball career when a bitter strike threatened to cancel that year's play. He showed he had not lost his touch when, in his third game back, he torched the New York Knicks for 55 points—the most points scored by anyone that season.

The Magic were able to hold Jordan in check for most of the series. In the first game, he shot only 8 for 22 and had the ball stolen in the closing seconds. "He looked over his left shoulder, but I was on the other side, and I got a hand on it and tipped it to Penny," Nick Anderson said. Hardaway and Jordan both lunged for the ball. Penny came up with it and flung a pass downcourt to a streaking Horace Grant who dunked it for the winning basket.

In Game 2, Jordan made a well-noticed change. He came on the court wearing his old number, 23. For all of this basketball season he wore 45, his baseball number, saying he had retired 23, the number his late father last saw him wearing. But when the Bulls needed a boost, he pulled out his old number, hoping it would pull out his old game-breaking skills. It seemed

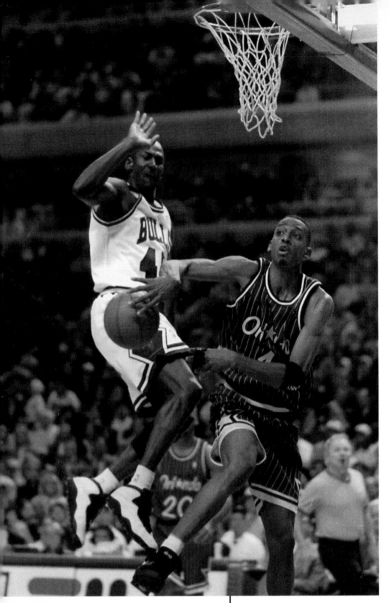

Hardaway fakes Michael Jordan into the air and then delivers a no-look pass as Orlando next took on the Chicago Bulls in the 1995 playoffs.

to work, as the Bulls knotted the series with a 104-94 win. (The league fined Jordan $25,000 for the unauthorized switch—a small price to pay given the size of the victory.)

Game 3 was Hardaway's day to shine. He scored 19 points, including the game-winning free throws. People had thought the Magic would have trouble winning on the road, but this 110-101 win in Chicago proved otherwise.

Penny had a subpar performance in Game 4, scoring only 16 points on 6 for 17 shooting as the Magic lost. The shorter B. J. Armstrong and Steve Kerr managed to keep Penny in check. Coach Brian Hill was chastised in the press for not utilizing Penny's height better.

Hardaway turned things around in a big way in Game 5. He had to leave the game at the end of the second quarter, when he reinjured his bruised left foot. But with three minutes remaining in the last quarter, he took the ball strong at Chicago's seven-foot-tall center Bill Wennington and unleashed a thunderous dunk that rocked the O-rena. The slam gave the Magic a 10-point lead they would hold easily to regain their advantage in the series.

Chicago was glad to be back on home turf for the sixth game of the series. The Bulls jumped out to a lead from the opening tip. Hardaway was one of the few Magic to play well in the first half. He scored 19 points in the first two quarters, keeping Orlando in the game almost single-handedly. Orlando started to trim Chicago's deficit a little in the third quarter, but with three minutes twenty-four seconds left in the game, the Bulls had a 102-94 lead.

Eight points is normally a solid lead with that amount of time remaining. But the Magic tightened their defense and shockingly did not allow Chicago to score any more points for the rest of the game. In that time, Michael Jordan looked very mortal, failing either to score himself or make the big play that freed up a teammate to score. Shaquille O'Neal showed his power and Nick Anderson sparkled in playing Jordan so tightly. The final horn put an end to Chicago's scoring drought—but by then, Orlando had gone on a 14-0 sprint. Final score: Orlando 108, Chicago 102. Teammates carried Horace Grant, the ex-Bull, off on their shoulders to celebrate their moving on in the playoffs.

The victory over Chicago proved that the Magic could take on any challenger. Hardaway and the rest of his teammates were pleased that their next challenger would be their old nemesis, the Indiana Pacers. The Pacers had just shocked the New York Knicks, pulling out a nail-biting series that went to the last second of the seventh and deciding game. Reggie Miller had been particularly effective. He personally stole a victory in the first game. The Knicks had a seemingly secure six-point lead with 18.7 seconds left in the game. But

Hardaway delivers a power dunk over Bulls center Bill Wennington as Michael Jordan looks on. The Magic ousted the Bulls in six games.

then Miller buried a three pointer, stole the inbounds pass, stepped behind the three-point line and fired. In 3.1 seconds, he had tied the game. After John Starks missed two free throws, Reggie got the ball back and was fouled. He hit both shots, and the Pacers had the edge they would need to get past the Knicks.

In Game 1 against Orlando, the Pacers jumped out to a 10-0 lead and continued on their way to a 23-5 lead in the first quarter. Reggie Miller sent a message that the Pacers were ready for the Magic, as he scored 12 of his team's first 13 points. The situation looked grim for Orlando, which had received unwelcome news earlier in the day, when the league announced that David Robinson of the San Antonio Spurs had won the MVP Award. Shaquille was second in the voting, and two other centers, Hakeem Olajuwon, the previous year's winner, and Patrick Ewing, were third and fourth. The announcement hardly pleased the league's top scorer in the regular season or his fans. "I'll get it one day," Shaq said. "They'll have to give it to me one day."

In the meantime, the Magic managed to find their composure. Hardaway announced Orlando's determination to fight back by dunking to start the second quarter. Three minutes, forty-six seconds later, they claimed their first lead. Indiana recovered to end the half up by a five-point margin, but that would not last long.

The Magic exploded in the third quarter, scoring 35 points. In a blistering 2 minutes, 17 seconds, Orlando went on a 12-point run that Penny ignited by hitting a jumper. He also hit two three pointers. When it was over, the Magic were 105-101 victors.

Hardaway also established the tone for Game 2. He came out smoking, hitting 11 points and handing out 5 assists in the first 12 minutes. Meantime, Reggie Miller made only 1 of 4 shots in the first quarter, as the Magic rolled up a 34-23 lead. Shaq played angry; he had shaved his head before the game because, he said, "I thought it would make me look more mean." It worked, as Shaq totaled 39 points, often dunking over Pacers center Rik Smits.

The Pacers won Game 3 as Coach Brian Hill protested that Shaq was fouled often but did not get the call. Shaq had only four foul shots in the game, an unusually low number for him.

In Game 4, Shaq again got in early foul trouble; he played only 30 minutes before fouling out and finished with only 16 points. Horace Grant fouled out even before Shaq, leaving the Magic with little of their famed inside game. But

Anfernee Hardaway came to Orlando's rescue, scoring a team-high 26 points and keeping the Magic in the game. In fact, the two teams played even up going into the final seconds.

And what an ending! "I've never seen a wilder 28 seconds than that," Pacer coach Larry Brown said of the tumultuous game's end. Brian Shaw started the clutch scoring with a bomb that put the Magic up by 1. The Pacers answered with a trey. Shaw buried another three pointer with 13.3 seconds left. Orlando 90, Indiana 89.

Reggie Miller hit a trey with 5.2 seconds left. Indiana 92, Orlando 90. The Magic called time-out. They called a play for their main man, hoping he could tie the score.

"I was supposed to go down and get the back cut along the baseline. But in my head, I wanted to go for the knockout punch," Penny said after the game.

And it looked like quite a knockout punch, too, as Penny stayed outside to hit a three pointer and give the Magic a 93-92 lead with a mere 1.3 seconds left on the game clock. One point three seconds is barely enough time to catch a long inbounds pass and immediately throw up a shot. But the Pacers called timeout in order to try to work a miracle.

The miracle worked. Rik Smits took the pass with Tree Rollins guarding him closely and fired from 16 feet. He got all net as the Pacers upheld their tradition of stealing close games.

"For all we did, there was still too much time left," said a stunned Hardaway after the game. "The end was just a shock. It just takes everything out of you."

Larry Brown had kind words for the Magic. "We're playing a very special team. They don't get rattled. They keep coming back at you."

Reggie Miller philosophized, "One point three seconds is a lifetime in this league. Our hearts are beating a little louder now. Where, if we were down 3-1, we probably wouldn't be heard."

The Pacers started hot in Game 5, played in Orlando. But Shaq was back on his game, and Brian Shaw by himself had an 8-0 run against Indiana. In the last seconds, as the Pacers again tried to steal the game, the Magic kept getting the ball in Hardaway's hands. And the Pacers kept fouling him. Penny went to the line three times in the last 30 seconds. He hit only two of his first four shots. But with 3.6 seconds left, he iced the game by hitting both foul shots, making the score 108-103. After the second shot went through the hoop, Penny raised his hands in celebration, accepting the cheering of the crowd. Reggie Miller hit another three at the buzzer, but it was too little, too late.

Now up three games to two in the series, the Magic looked to advance by winning Game 6 in Indiana. So far, each team had won when on its home court, but the Pacers' history of pulling out last-minute miracles—even on an opponent's turf—was not lost on Orlando.

The Pacers blew out to a 27-point lead in the first half, and this time they never looked back. They ballooned the lead to 35 several times in the second half. Previously, no game had been decided by more than 5 points. The Magic would have to regroup fast and forget about this game if they were going to have a chance in the deciding game. Mark Jackson, a Pacer point guard, tried to put extra heat on the Magic by going to the press and guaranteeing an Indiana victory.

Hardaway dashes to the basket, leaving Dale Davis of the Indiana Pacers grasping at air. The Magic defeated their nemesis in seven tough games in the 1995 playoffs.

This was the Magic's biggest test—by far. All year long, people had been questioning their experience and ability to play well in tough situations. Now, in a winner-take-all situation, the youngest team in the NBA wanted to show that they could shake off one poor outing and win the big one.

And Orlando had just the player to lead them: Penny Hardaway. The Magic jumped out to a lead in the first quarter and never let Indiana back in the game. Hardaway finished with 17 points, including several key three pointers as Orlando hit a stunning 13 of 17 shots from beyond the arc.

Again, Penny's performance cannot be summed up adequately by looking at the score sheet. In the third quarter, Orlando went on a 13-1 run which effectively buried the Pacers' chances. Penny was responsible for much of the run, playing total team ball. He saw Horace Grant open at the post and whipped him a pass, forcing Rik Smits to commit his third foul and sending him to the bench.

He found Nick Anderson on the left wing, and Anderson spotted up for a three pointer. Penny reached in to steal the ball from Antonio Davis, then passed to Shaq for a dunk. Penny stole another ball as a bewildered Pacer thought he had a sure two points; Penny then sent another bullet pass crosscourt to Dennis Scott who launched yet another successful trey. Viewers on court, in the arena, and those all around the country watching on television had to be reminded of the best players they had seen before—marvels such as Magic Johnson, Larry Bird, and Michael Jordan.

Meantime, Reggie Miller had a poor game, hitting only 5 of 13 shots for a grand total of 12 points for the game. The Magic humiliated the Pacers, routing them 105-81.

"Everyone kept saying we didn't have the experience, we couldn't go all the way," said Penny emotionally after the game. "It motivated us, it really did. While everybody was criticizing, we just kept playing ball."

"If we played our best game, I don't think we would have won with the way they played tonight," Larry Brown analyzed afterward. "They had great performances from everybody....It hurts when you get it so close, to a seventh game. But the best team won."

After the final horn sounded, the Orlando Arena went crazy. Fireworks exploded and streamers came down from the rafters. Magic players hugged as a delirious crowd danced onto the court. Shaq lifted Coach Hill into the air and put him on his shoulders.

Orlando had beaten their nemesis and gone from no playoff wins to 11 playoff wins—and a chance to play for the NBA championship.

6

STILL LEARNING

Orlando's opponent in the 1995 NBA finals was the Houston Rockets. The Rockets were the defending champions, but for a long time they did not seem like the same team that had defeated the New York Knicks in the finals the year before. In 1994, the Rockets destroyed all their competition throughout the year, but 1995 was another story. They struggled early and although they ended strongly, they still finished only fifth in their division. No team had ever started so far down in the standings and ended up winning the championship.

In hard-fought series, the Rockets defeated the Utah Jazz, Phoenix Suns, and San Antonio Spurs. They entered the championship round having won seven consecutive away games.

Houston's Hakeem Olajuwon was one of the most intriguing players in the NBA. The Nigerian-born star grew up playing soccer. At 6'10"

Coach Brian Hill (to Hardaway's left) draws up a play during a timeout in the 1995 championship series.

The strong play of Sam Cassell was a major reason why the Houston Rockets were able to outplay the Magic and win their second consecutive championship in 1995.

and unusually coordinated, Olajuwon learned basketball at the University of Houston, where he and Clyde Drexler formed the nucleus of a high-flying troop that became known as Phi Slamma Jamma. In the 1984 draft, the Houston Rockets made Olajuwon the number one pick. The Chicago Bulls made Michael Jordan the number three pick.

All the world was looking to watch the matchup of Olajuwon versus O'Neal. As it turned out, the head-to-head meetings were pretty much even, with Olajuwon outscoring O'Neal and O'Neal out-rebounding Olajuwon by fairly narrow margins. The championship turned out to hinge on the rest of the starters and the bench.

The first game saw the Magic rush out to an early lead. For much of the contest they were up by 20 points, but then the Rockets came clawing back. Kenny Smith hit 6 three pointers to tie a record. Still, the Magic seemed to have the game locked up when they held a 110-107 advantage with 10.5 seconds left in the game and Nick Anderson shooting two free throws. Anderson missed both shots but grabbed the offensive rebound on his second miss. He was fouled with just under eight seconds remaining and received two more shots to ice the game. He missed them both.

Houston still needed a small miracle, and they got it. The Rockets rebounded Anderson's final miss, and the ball wound up in the hands of Kenny Smith. He gave a head fake to Anfernee Hardaway and hit a three pointer that set a new record and sent the game into overtime.

With only seconds left in the overtime and the score tied at 118, Clyde Drexler took a running shot. Shaq went to challenge it and the shot bounced off the rim, and Olajuwon was there to tap it in with .03 seconds left on the game clock. The Rockets took Game 1.

Anderson played poorly for the rest of the series, and his teammates seemed to suffer his embarrassment as well. Meantime, Robert Horry, Kenny Smith, and Sam Cassell played basketball at a level few fans knew to expect of them. The Rockets rolled over the Magic 117-106 in Game 2.

Game 3 was played in Houston, and Anfernee Hardaway did all he could to get the Magic back into the swing. He scored 19 points and passed out 14 assists, and he got help from Shaq, who had 28 points with 12 rebounds. But with 14.1 seconds left and Houston up by 101-100, Robert Horry launched an amazing three pointer. Orlando requested a timeout and called a play for Penny.

Penny received the ball and desperately threw up a shot from way beyond the three-point line;

it missed the rim by a good two feet. He thought he was fouled, but the referee did not blow his whistle. Houston won, 105-103.

When asked if the Magic did not have enough experience to win the title, Penny explained, "I don't think we believed that when the series started. I guess people will say that now."

The fourth game was a foregone conclusion. No one had ever recovered from a 0-3 margin in the finals of a basketball championship, and the Magic were not about to become the first. With Olajuwon playing as well as a human can and Sam Cassell doing a remarkable job of shutting down Hardaway, the Rockets swept the Magic.

As the Houston fans whooped and hollered after the game was over, the Magic did not retreat quickly to their dressing rooms, as the losing team traditionally does. Coach Brian Hill gathered his troops around him and urged them to take a good look around, to drink in the moment. Anfernee Hardaway looked around at the celebration he could not join. As a child of the ghetto, Penny knew that no one could promise him that he would ever get to win a championship. No one, that is, besides himself.

Penny inwardly vowed to be back in the finals one day. And with his skills, and the skills of his teammates, it is a very good bet that he will make good on that promise.

STATISTICS

ANFERNEE DEON HARDAWAY

Year	Team	G	FGA	FGM	PCT	FTA	FTM	PCT	REB	AST	PTS	AVG
1991–92	MSU	34	483	209	.433	158	103	.652	237	188	590	17.4
1992–93	MSU	32	522	249	.477	206	158	.767	273	204	729	22.8
Total		66	1005	458	.456	364	261	.717	510	392	1319	20.0
1993–94	Orl	82	1092	509	.486	330	245	.742	439	544	1313	18.7
1994–95	Orl	77	1142	585	.512	463	356	.769	336	551	1613	20.9
Total		159	2234	1094	.490	793	601	.758	775	1095	2928	18.4

G	game
FGA	field goals attempted
FGM	field goals made
PCT	percent
FTA	free throws attempted
FTM	free throws made
REB	rebounds
AST	assists
PTS	points
AVG	scoring average

ANFERNEE HARDAWAY
A CHRONOLOGY

1972   Anfernee Hardaway born in Memphis, Tennessee, July 18

1978   Fae Hardaway leaves for California; Anfernee is thereafter raised by his grandmother, Louise Hardaway

1990   Anfernee Hardaway named one of 10 best high school basketball players by *Sporting News*; because Penny scores under 18 on the ACTs, he becomes ineligible to play college ball; during a robbery, he is shot in the foot

1991   Since bringing his grades up at Memphis State University, Hardaway becomes eligible to play ball

1992   Hardaway scrimmages with the U.S. Olympic "Dream" Team and makes fans out of Magic Johnson and Larry Bird; brings home a gold medal from the Olympic Festival

1993   After winning two consecutive Great Midwest Player of the Year awards, Hardaway announces he will turn pro; the Golden State Warriors use their third pick in the draft to select him and immediately trade him and future draft picks to the Orlando Magic for their number one selection, Chris Webber

1994   Leads Orlando to its first postseason appearance

1995   Hardaway is named to the All-Star Game; leads Orlando to the championship series where they are beaten by the Houston Rockets

SUGGESTIONS FOR FURTHER READING

Howerton, Darryl. "The Jordan Heirs." *Sport*, March, 1995.

Starr, Mark. "This Penny is Worth Millions." *Newsweek*, March, 1993.

Taylor, Phil. "Together Forever." *Sports Illustrated*, February 4, 1994.

Wiley, Ralph. "A Daunting Proposition: A Year as Prop 48 Athlete is Humbling, but Anfernee Hardaway Made the Grade." *Sports Illustrated*, August 12, 1991.

ABOUT THE AUTHOR

Jeremy Daniels has a degree in English from Trinity College in Hartford, Connecticut. He has spent 18 years in publishing as an editor, writer, and translator. Daniels is the author of *All Sorts of Sports*, published by Holt, Rinehart & Winston.

INDEX

64